Public School Purpose: The Civic Standard

by
Merle Steven McClung

ISBN 0-87367-885-0
Copyright © 2002 by the Phi Delta Kappa Educational Foundation
Bloomington, Indiana

Table of Contents

Table of Contents

Introduction

In 2000, the U.S. Supreme Court essentially decided who would be our 43rd president. The media quickly dubbed this "our national civics lesson." The lesson was not only about what structural changes might be necessary to prevent a recurrence of this problem, but also about a citizen's responsibility as a voter in our democracy. Almost one-half of eligible voters had not even bothered to vote, and hundreds of thousands who did vote had invalidated their own ballots by casting them improperly. This failure of one-half of our citizens to vote, or to vote effectively, reflects a marked decline in civic participation (Putnam 2000).

Before these serious civic issues could be addressed, a second national civics lesson suddenly upstaged the first. On 11 September 2001, international terrorists hijacked and crashed commercial airliners into the World Trade Center and the Pentagon, killing thousands of civilians. Americans responded with a great deal of flag-waving and a new spirit of patriotism, and they raised disturbing questions about whether the U.S. Constitution underpinning our free and open society at the same time undermined our security. Core values of our con-

7

stitutional democracy were called into question: Could we afford to guarantee the very constitutional freedoms that seemed to make us vulnerable — or could we afford not to?

These challenges to our democracy came at a time when there has been a widespread public perception that our schools are failing to teach students basic skills. Politicians forced an extensive and controversial standards and testing movement on a skeptical education establishment, and some even called for a new mission for public education to help deal with the unique challenges of a new century.

However, before embracing a new purpose for schools in the 21st century, we should consider the purpose that is rooted in our history. Simply stated, the primary purpose of public education is to prepare students to participate effectively as citizens in our constitutional democracy. That is "the civic standard."

By incorporating the core values of our democracy, the civic standard provides general and specific direction for public education. It is the ultimate standard and the one that should be used to evaluate our schools. Just as the U.S. Constitution provides direction for our country, the civic standard can provide direction for public education. This fastback is a preliminary attempt to define and interpret the civic standard.

The Civic Standard

Many people argue that the primary purpose of public education is to prepare students for college or a job. But that is not the vision of education that the Founding Fathers proposed. They had a broader purpose in mind.

Consider, for example, George Washington in his Farewell Address of 1796: "Promote then, as an object of importance, institutions for the general diffusion of knowledge. In proportion as the structure of government gives force to public opinion, it is essential that public opinion should be enlightened." Thomas Jefferson wrote: "It is an axiom in my mind that our liberty can never be safe but in the hands of the people themselves, and that too of the people with a certain degree of instruction." Similarly, John Adams wrote, "Education is more indispensable, and must be more general under a free government than any other." Consider also the words of Benjamin Franklin: "We must have a system of public education; its purpose must be to educate our people in their public duties."

Cressman and Benda review the writings of these and other founders and conclude: "the founders were firm in their belief that any system of education, particularly at public expense, would have as its fundamental purpose that of making the new government work" (1960, p. 6). The exact words may differ, but the basic concept of the founders is the same: The primary purpose of public education in the United States is to prepare students to participate effectively as citizens in our constitutional democracy.

There were differences among the nation's founders that did not end with the ratification of the Constitution. The central conflict between Jeffersonian Republicanism, emphasizing decentralized individual liberty, and Hamiltonian Federalism, emphasizing centralized collectivism, continues today within that constitutional framework. The founders gave us something more important than some final resolution of differences. They gave us some core values that could be applied to changing circumstances and a framework within which to continue the debate and to seek better solutions.

The central conflict between the conservative and progressive traditions in public education also can be continued within a common framework of core values while encouraging continued debate. Rather than emphasizing our differences, the civic standard emphasizes our common values by providing a primary goal and common framework within which to seek better solutions.

The Multipurpose Abyss

Unfortunately, the civic standard was never carefully defined or implemented. Eventually it was lost as meaningless rhetoric among multiple goals designed to appease diverse constituencies. Consider, for example, the Seven Cardinal Principles that the 1918 Commission on the Reorganization of Secondary Education (CRSE) proposed as the main objectives of secondary education: Health, Command of Fundamental Processes, Worthy Home Membership, Vocation, Citizenship, Worthy Use of Leisure, and Ethical Character.

Countless variations of such multipurpose standards have been articulated throughout the 20th century without any attempt to prioritize, much less define them. Even when schools attempt to identify specific criteria beyond such goal statements, Theodore Sizer notes: "the result has been lists of daunting pseudospecificity and numbing earnestness. However, most [schools] leave the words undefined and let the momentum of traditional practice speak for itself" (Sizer 1984, p. 78). Given the often disputatious constituencies involved in public education, some conclude that a unifying primary purpose is either unworkable or undesirable.

Although a multipurpose approach is politically and educationally easier to achieve, it precludes a clear sense of purpose and priority that is at least partly responsible for public school problems throughout the 20th century. A preferable approach for the 21st century would encourage states and schools to find the best ways to achieve the civic standard.

According to Diane Ravitch, multiple goals reflect the loss of the public school compass that occurred when progressivism overwhelmed the academic curriculum. Once schools lost their sense of academic mission, "education reform movements would come and go with surprising rapidity. . . . Every purveyor of social reform could find a willing customer in the schools because all needs were presumed equal in importance, and there was no longer any general consensus on the central purpose of schooling" (Ravitch 2000, pp. 16-17).

However, Ravitch's proposed primary academic purpose conflicts in both theory and practice with the civic standard. So, too, does the primary economic purpose that is assumed by the current standards and accountability movement. As underscored by Marc Tucker, "The problem to which the [standards and accountability] movement was a response was posed by a swiftly integrating world economy and the need for higher-skilled workers" (Tucker 2002, p. 76). While our market economy has created one of the highest standards of living in the world and is a valued part of our system, that does not mean its priorities should prevail in our public schools. The founders did not conceive the primary purpose of public education to be to train students to function as efficient workers, and neither should we.

In framing and implementing education policy, the economic and academic purposes should be considered as secondary and must advance, or at least not obstruct, the primary civic purpose. The standards and accountability movement may set multiple standards at many levels in public schools, but they should be designed and implemented around the primary civic standard.

The civic standard is not very useful when it is used only for its rhetorical value. Fortunately, some educators and some courts have moved beyond the rhetoric to examine the meaning and implications of the civic standard in the kind of detail that provides helpful direction.

Defining the Civic Standard

Theodore Sizer asks what learning the state can properly demand of its citizens. Sizer outlines three minimal requirements of the civic standard: literacy, numeracy, and civic understanding.

Literacy implies clear thought; that is, one must read easily and sensitively enough to comprehend at least the basic arguments presented by contemporary political and social life. Without that ability and the correlative ability to present such arguments oneself orally and in clear writing, a citizen cannot fully participate in a democracy.

Numeracy means the ability to use numbers, arithmetically and algebraically, and to understand the concepts, relationships, and logic embedded in mathematical thought. A modern citizen cannot make critical judgments without these skills.

Civic understanding means a grasp of the basis for consensual democratic government, a respect for its processes, and acceptance of the restraints and obligations incumbent on a citizen. These restraints and obligations are eloquently summarized in the Bill of Rights. (Sizer 1984, p. 88)

Sizer argues that compulsory education should be limited to up to eighth grade because "most young citizens should master those minima before senior high school." In fact, too many students do not master such minima in 12 years — resulting in today's standards and accountability movement, as well as a proliferation of college remedial programs. While the state could lower the compulsory education age and permit earlier access to the workforce, less education for our most needy children does not seem advisable. Furthermore, the minimal requirements should not limit the civic standard if more can be accomplished in 12 years.

The civic standard is not easily achieved. As Gelhorn and Byse emphasize: "A constitutional democracy like ours is perhaps the most difficult of man's social arrangements to manage successfully. Our scheme of society is more dependent than any other form of government on knowledge and wisdom and self-discipline for the achievement of its aims. For our democracy implies the reign of reason on the most extensive scale" (Gelhorn and Byse 1960, p. 83).

The complexity of our constitutional democracy does not mean that everyone needs to be a constitutional scholar to participate effectively, but surely the civic standard provides sufficient substance to challenge even the best students for 12 years.

In her influential book, *Democratic Education*, Amy Gutmann provides what is perhaps the most careful and extensive examination of a comparable citizenship concept. Gutmann sees the primary purpose of public education as the preparation of students for democratic citizenship, including the capacity to participate effectively in American politics. Gutmann outlines what she would consider the minimum requirements necessary to make a liberal democracy work fairly: "the civic minimum would include teaching not only the 3R's but also religious toleration and nondiscrimination, racial and gender nondiscrimination, respect for individual rights and legitimate laws, the ability to articulate and the courage to stand up for one's publicly defensible convictions, the ability to deliberate with others and therefore to be open-minded about politically relevant issues, and the ability to evaluate the performance of officeholders" (Gutmann 1999, p. 298).

Gutmann's theory of democratic education is grounded in "those principles — of non-repression and non-discrimination — that preserve the intellectual and social foundations of democratic deliberations." Gutmann proceeds with the difficult task of applying these principles to a broad range of controversial school issues, such as censorship, creationism, racial and sex discrimination, school finance, vouchers, etc. In doing so, she provides a detailed analysis of the meaning of democratic education and makes no apology for its political purpose. "Political education — the cultivation of the virtues, knowledge, and skills necessary for political participation — has moral primacy over other purposes of public education in a democratic society. Political education prepares citizens to participate in consciously reproducing their society" (1999, p. 287). Political participation is key for Gutmann, who argues, "If primary schooling leaves students with a capacity for political criticism but no capacity for political participation or sense of social commitment, either because it fails to cultivate their sense of political efficacy or because it succeeds in teaching them deference to authority, then it will have neglected to cultivate a virtue essential to democracy" (1999, p. 92).

Applying the logic of democratic education to the content and process of public education, Gutmann concludes, "the primacy of political education supplies a principled argument against tracking, sexist education, racial segregation, and (narrowly) vocational education. Even when these practices improve the academic achievement of students, they neglect the virtues of citizenship, which can be cultivated by a common education characterized by respect for racial, religious, intellectual and sexual differences among students" (1999, p. 286).

Gutmann's construct of democratic education is distinguishable from the civic standard proposed in this fastback because her construct is "universally," rather than nationally, based. Gutmann's analysis is not based primarily on the U.S. Constitution and the history of our constitutional democracy, but on her definition of nonrepression and nondiscrimination as constraints on majority rule. Therefore her construct is extended easily to postsecondary and other forms of education and to comparable issues in other democracies.

The civic standard in this fastback derives its support from the history of public education in our constitutional democracy. Therefore the analysis and extent of the civic standard is limited to publicly funded U.S.

elementary and secondary education — specifically the 12 years of compulsory education.

Our history provides strong support for the civic standard, but much of this support is mostly just rhetoric. Therefore the task is to translate the concept of the civic standard into concrete, workable direction and content for schools.

Sizer and Gutmann provide two answers to this question, and they can be considered as opposite ends of a minima-maxima spectrum of the meaning of education for citizenship in our democracy. Many "civic minimalists" would contend that Sizer's minima is not sufficiently minimal; but, to the extent that they would achieve consensus by narrowing the scope of open discussion and debate within the classroom, they are inconsistent with the civic standard. So, too, some "civic maximalists" might argue that Gutmann's maxima is not sufficiently maximal; but that extension of the spectrum at some point would be inconsistent with the civic standard. Such postmodernists as Henry Giroux and Paulo Freire, for example, often are criticized for their unabashed indoctrination of students.

While most of Sizer's requirements are quantifiable and measurable by standardized tests, the most important part of Gutmann's requirements are not. The participatory, persuasive, and interpersonal skills that are a central part of her requirements are intangible or behavioral and are evaluated best by the observation and judgment of the classroom teacher.

The primary purpose of public education should not be limited by what is quantifiable, especially when that primary purpose also focuses on participatory values. The civic standard specifically emphasizes effective participation as citizens. The student who can score best on a standardized or teacher-prepared test that measures knowledge of participation is not necessarily the best at effective participation.

Standardized tests cannot measure much of what the civic standard considers valuable. In selecting his staff and cabinet, the President does not give standardized tests to applicants to determine the best-qualified citizens for the positions. That would be patently absurd. But if this is so clear in the adult world, why should schools focus primarily on quantifiable skills, and why should standardized tests determine if a student gets a diploma? Such use of testing makes sense for assessing the quantifiable part of the civic standard, and it may be defensible given some concepts of academics as the primary purpose; but it distorts a key part of what is considered important in the civic standard.

Although it may create special problems for assessment and judicial review, the civic standard should not be defined in minimum terms. The civic standard should represent the maximum that can be achieved within the 12 years of compulsory education.

The Law and the Civic Standard

This oft-quoted dictum about educational purpose in *Brown* v. *Board of Education* still resonates today:

> Today, education is perhaps the most important function of state and local governments. Compulsory school attendance laws and the great expenditures for education both demonstrate our recognition of the importance of education to our democratic society. It is required in the performance of our most basic public responsibilities, even service in the armed forces. It is the very foundation of good citizenship. (*Brown* v. *Board of Education*, 347 U.S. 483 [1954], p. 493)

The U.S. Supreme Court has played a major role in defining the values that are implicit in the civic standard. To take just one particularly eloquent example from a decade before *Brown*, consider former Supreme Court Justice Robert H. Jackson's points in a case overturning a compulsory flag salute in *West Virginia Board of Education* v. *Barnette*:

> The Fourteenth Amendment, as now applied to the States, protects the citizen against the State itself and all of its creatures — Boards of Education not excepted.

These have, of course, important, delicate, and highly discretionary functions, but none that they may not perform within the limits of the Bill of Rights. That they are educating the young for citizenship is reason for scrupulous protection of the Constitutional freedoms of the individual, if we are not to strangle the free mind at its source and teach youth to discount important principles as mere platitudes. (*Barnette*, p. 493)

Justice Jackson proceeded to distinguish between free and compelled belief: "freedom to differ is not limited to things that do not matter much. That would be a mere shadow of freedom. The test of its substance is the right to differ as to things that touch the heart of the existing order. If there is any fixed star in our Constitutional constellation, it is that no official, high or petty, can prescribe what shall be orthodox in politics, nationalism, religion, or other matters of opinion or force citizens to confess by word or act their faith therein."

Constitutional provisions evolve over time, and subsequent Supreme Court decisions have afforded states and local school authorities more discretion to determine education policy. Consider, for example, *San Antonio Independent School District* v. *Rodriguez*, overturning a district court decision that a Texas school finance system allowing severe inequities between poor and rich districts violated the Fourteenth Amendment's equal protection guarantee. In a 5-4 decision, Justice Powell for the majority did not dispute the Hispanic plaintiffs' claim that education is essential to free speech and participation in the political process:

Exercise of the franchise, it is contended, cannot be divorced from the educational foundation of the voter.

The electoral process, if reality is to conform to the democratic ideal, depends on an informed electorate: a voter cannot cast his ballot intelligently unless his reading skills and thought processes have been adequately developed. (*Rodriguez*, p. 35)

Although stating, "We need not dispute any of these propositions," the majority concluded that education is not a fundamental interest for purposes of equal protection analysis and that the state's claim of providing an adequate education for every child had not been disproved. Justice Powell also indicated concern not only about the difficulty of developing a judicially manageable standard to define and enforce some identifiable quantum of education as the prerequisite to the meaningful exercise of the right, but also "the controversy as to the proper goals of the system of public education" (*Rodriguez*, p. 42).

Federal courts in general have been reluctant to elaborate on the purpose of public education beyond dicta that usually reiterate the rhetoric of the civic standard. It is not federal but state courts — in the context of school finance litigation under state education clauses — that in recent years have provided a legal dimension and specific meaning to statements of educational purpose.

State Courts and Justice DeGrasse's Decision

One of the most extensive examinations of a comparable civic standard is provided by Justice Leland DeGrasse in *Campaign for Fiscal Equity* v. *State of New*

York, the case challenging the adequacy of the state's system of school finance for New York City school children. Justice DeGrasse's task is to interpret and implement the following template for "a sound basic education" handed down by the New York Court of Appeals:

> the opportunity to acquire the basic literacy, calculating and verbal skills necessary to enable [students] to function as civic participants capable of voting and serving as jurors. (*Campaign for Fiscal Equity* v. *State*, 655 N.E.2d 661 [NY 1995])

While Justice DeGrasse somewhat implausibly found employment and higher education goals inherent in this civic template, his related analysis of "productive citizenship" and "civic engagement" is instructive. Since a template is a guide, rather than the thing itself, the court saw "voting and jury service as synecdoches for the larger concept of productive citizenship.... Productive citizenship means more than just being qualified to vote and serve as a juror, but to do so capably and knowledgeably" (*CFE* v. *State*, 719 N.Y.S.2d 475 [N.Y. Sup. Ct. 2001], p. 485).

Although Justice DeGrasse emphasizes that voting and jury service are only examples of the larger concept of productive citizenship, he analyzes the skills necessary for these specific civic tasks. For example, with respect to voting, DeGrasse writes:

> An engaged, capable voter needs the intellectual tools to evaluate complex issues, such as campaign finance reform, tax policy, and global warming, to name

only a few. Ballot propositions in New York City, such as the charter reform proposal that was on the ballot in November 1999, can require a close reading and a familiarity with the structure of local government. (p. 487)

And with respect to jury service as well as voting, note that Justice DeGrasse also lists skills that require good participatory and judgmental skills, as well as traditional linguistic and logical skills:

> Similarly, a capable and productive citizen doesn't simply show up for jury service. Rather she is capable of serving impartially on trials that may require learning unfamiliar facts and concepts and new ways to communicate and reach decisions with her fellow jurors. To be sure, the jury is in some respects an anti-elitist institution where life experience and practical intelligence can be more important than formal education. Nonetheless, jurors may be called on to decide complex matters that require the verbal, reasoning, math, science, and socialization skills that should be imparted in public schools. Jurors today must determine questions of fact concerning DNA evidence, statistical analyses, and convoluted financial fraud, to name only three topics (p. 485).

The cognitive skills identified by Justice DeGrasse are "high-order" skills that go far beyond the minimum 3R's. By tying cognitive skills to the complex voter and jury functions of contemporary civic life, the court raised the bar for what is considered an adequate education.

DeGrasse's definition of education adequacy created a formidable, some would say impossible, task for schools. However, this tougher definition forms a worthy goal if it is not also tied to diploma denial. The court did not set minimum standards that schools must achieve to be considered adequate, only the opportunity to achieve them. However, one concern is that some schools might be tempted to use these high-order cognitive skills as a requirement for high school graduation.

The language of the New York template is similar to that of the civic standard in that it incorporates an active participatory value, as well as the necessary cognitive skills. The communication and socialization skills cited by DeGrasse are difficult, if not impossible, to quantify but are consistent with the reality that voter and jury decisions, like most important decisions in the real world, ultimately involve judgment calls. Reflecting the real world in which citizens engage and participate, the civic standard values both the cognitive and non-cognitive, the scientific and the judgmental, the tangible and the intangible, the quantifiable and non-quantifiable. For ease of discussion throughout this fastback, these dichotomies can be simplified as "cognitive skills" and "participatory values."

This dichotomy between cognitive skills and participatory values presents a basic dilemma for the courts because it is easier to fashion an order or remedy around cognitive skills that can be assessed by traditional standardized tests. In fact, Michael Rebell (2002) underscores the crucial connection between the Standards Movement with its quantifiable standards and such "third wave" adequacy decisions as *CFE* v. *State*. If comparable weight is given to both cognitive skills and participatory values, how should the latter be assessed and how would alternative assessment methods affect the justiciability of such cases? On the other hand, if all or most of the emphasis is given to cognitive skills because they can be more easily assessed by traditional measures, participatory values are likely to be shortchanged. Therefore the civic standard cannot be fully implemented in New York or elsewhere without the cooperation and "civic engagement" of the relevant legislative bodies and, ultimately, of the schools and other stakeholders in public education.

In a 3-1 decision on 25 June 2002, a New York Appellate Division panel held that Justice DeGrasse's interpretation of the civic template is too broad because the test should be not whether the public schools prepare a student for "competitive employment," but for any self-supporting job at all (the equivalent of an eighth- or ninth-grade education). As the *CFE* plaintiffs have appealed this decision, the New York Court of Appeals will have the opportunity to further define the civic standard set forth in its template.

Implications of the Civic Standard

The civic standard has other important implications for the content, process, and assessment of public education. The starting point on content is a basic knowledge of how citizens govern themselves in our constitutional democracy: its core values, how they translate in practice, how that practice differs from the ideal, whether the system (including its core values) or the practice should be changed, and the means by which our democracy provides for change and resolution of conflicting ideas.

There are, of course, many ways in which this basic knowledge can be taught, ways that probably are best left to the discretion of the classroom teacher. For example, the issues posed in the preceding paragraph could be addressed with respect to the 2000 presidential election, frequently referred to as "our national civics lesson." What core values does the Electoral College protect? Would a simple popular vote or other change better protect these values? If so, how can this change be accomplished? A teacher might stimulate this discussion with a deliberately provocative hypothesis, such as: "Usually, the President appoints Supreme Court Justices. But this constitutional procedure was reversed in the 2000 Election. Do you agree? Be sure to support your conclusion with reasons you are prepared to defend."

The 2000 election provides many other lessons. For example, a teacher might develop lessons on the U.S. Attorney General's Office proposed lawsuit against Florida, Missouri, and Tennessee for discriminatory treatment of minority voters and how those aggrieved voters were able to force this action. Similarly, teachers could and probably are developing many instructive lessons out of our "Second National Civics Lesson," focusing on whether 21st century terror tactics justify new restrictions on privacy and other constitutional rights.

The Bill of Rights provides a rich source of core values that directly affect the lives of students. What implications do various provisions of the Bill of Rights have for how students treat each other, their teachers, their parents, and citizens in general? What responsibilities correspond to rights provided by our Constitution? How do the rights of adult citizens differ from those of citizens who are elementary and secondary students being trained for citizenship? What time, place, and manner restrictions are necessary?

Sizer would engage students with similar questions directly affecting their lives. Should girls be drafted and play the same roles as boys do in military service? The effect of cliques, such as jocks, preps, freaks, brains, and even smokers, on their classmates, school, and community become a legitimate source of classroom discussion

(Sizer 1984, pp. 26-27). Using provocative contemporary topics to teach participatory and critical-thinking skills has been an effective pedagogical tool used by teachers for decades (McClung 1970).

For Ravitch, resorting to current issues that have general social significance and appeal to a student's immediate interests are part of the dumbed-down curriculum created by the "social studies" courses that displaced such traditional academic courses on ancient, European, English, and American history (Ravitch 2000, p. 127). She urges a return to an academic model. But does it really matter much if the subject is William Jefferson Clinton instead of Thomas Jefferson, or the 2000 presidential election instead of the one in 1800? The critical-thinking skills developed in this participatory context can be as rigorous as traditional academic study, as evidenced by the Socratic method still used by most law schools. These lessons are more consistent with the participatory values of the civic standard, which necessarily emphasizes current issues that have general social significance. Few would contend that historical perspective is not important, but rigor has less to do with *what* than with *how* a subject is taught. Teaching to memorize a bunch of dates and other facts, whether contemporary or historical, is less rigorous than teaching critical analysis of those facts in context.

If the civic standard represents the primary purpose of public education, a course or two in government or civics obviously cannot achieve it. The civic standard must extend beyond such courses; it should permeate all curricular and extracurricular learning in a school.

At its core, the civic standard is as much about process as it is about content. No matter how well a school teaches content, what it practices often is more instructive for students. Noncurricular practices send strong messages; they are "the hidden curriculum." Rote learning, compelled belief, and authoritarian methods will not advance the critical thinking and open discussion of ideas that are central to the civic standard.

Consider a more controversial example of the hidden curriculum in schools. Students tend to segregate themselves into self-appointed cliques for security, image, and other reasons; but public schools should not reinforce these limiting stereotypes. While the underlying causes of the shootings at Columbine High School were no doubt complex, one of the most frequent explanations given by students in the aftermath of the tragedy was the bullying of the "freaks" by the "jocks." Related reports emphasized the sometimes abusive arrogance of the athletes and the school's role in reinforcing this attitude by an overemphasis on the school's athletic programs.

Learning to understand and deal with diversity obviously is not facilitated by segregating students by any trait. Because of the importance of the civic standard, the justification for ability grouping of social studies and English classes is less apparent than for science and math.

The injurious effects of state-sponsored racial segregation have been documented extensively (Ryan 1999). But segregation of students into separate schools and classrooms by almost any trait can have harmful effects.

Consider another controversial example: segregation by sex. The most common rationale for single-sex schools and classes is that girls will do better academically if they are not distracted by what the boys might think about their academic aspirations. This is an important goal if one assumes that the primary purpose of schools is academic. But the civic standard's emphasis on participatory values would take precedence even if studies conclusively showed that girls did better academically in single-sex schools. Even if girls performed better academically, the more relevant question is whether participatory learning suffers.

Similarly, what is the impact of single-sex classes and schools on boys? As emphasized by Susan Bailey: "[There are] critical aspects of social development that our culture has traditionally assigned to women that are equally important to men. Schools must help girls *and* boys acquire both the relational and the competitive skills needed for full participation in the workforce, family, and community" (Bailey and AAUW 1995, p. 4). Although this assumes the kind of tripartite purpose for schools that is questioned in this fastback, the suggestion here is that single-sex schools and classes do not serve *any* of these purposes.

The civic standard also has important implications for home schooling. Home schooling may be the best solution for some children with highly specialized needs, but the presumption should be that substantial isolation from other children and activities is inconsistent with the civic standard. Some parents and some home tutors may succeed in teaching the requisite cognitive skills, but it is difficult to imagine comparable success with participatory skills.

Some Assessment Implications

Because the civic standard calls for both cognitive skills and participatory values, it requires an assessment that goes beyond standardized testing to include assessment of nonquantitative, participatory values. The interpersonal and social skills involved in the civic standard are demonstrable, but they are not measurable by traditional tests. Thus the evaluation of a student's, teacher's, or school's success with the civic standard also requires careful and considered judgment calls.

We must avoid the error of thinking something is important simply because it can be quantified. Even in our test- and number-obsessed nation, most citizens would appreciate the wisdom of the old saw attributed to Albert Einstein: "Not everything that can be measured counts, and not everything that counts can be measured." So, too, as Antoine de Saint-Exupéry's Little Prince might put it: "We can find the essential if we try / To see what's invisible to the eye."

Howard Gardner argues that our society puts too much emphasis on two kinds of intelligence, linguistic intelligence and logical-mathematical intelligence, partly because language and logic lend themselves to traditional paper-and-pencil tests. Gardner contends that at least five other kinds of intelligence of equal value are ignored or shortchanged: spatial, musical, bodily-kinesthetic, interpersonal, and intrapersonal. Of these, interpersonal intelligence is the most relevant to the civic standard. Gardner defines interpersonal intelligence as "the ability to understand other people: what motivates them, how they work, how to work cooperatively with them" (Gardner 1993, p. 9). Gardner and his colleagues have been working to develop a fair means of assessing intelligence by using such contextualized vehicles as student projects and process folios.

Some attempts to "quantify" participatory values have been unimpressive, such as the simplistic "time-on-task" assessment of its community service program reportedly made by one school: one hour a week of community service earns a C, two hours a B, three or more hours an A. Such crude measures reinforce the argument that good measures do not exist for alternative assessment.

When you know something is important, you don't dismiss it because it is difficult to evaluate. Consider the recent trend in the corporate world to develop alternative assessments for market value and personnel evaluation. Marcus Buckingham and Curt Coffman argue that today's investors and corporations know that their current measuring sticks do a very poor job of capturing important sources of a company's value: "whether software designer or delivery truck driver, accountant or hotel housekeeper, the most valuable aspects of jobs are now, as Thomas Stewart described in *Intellectual Capital*, 'the most essentially human tasks: sensing, judging, creating, and building relationships'" (Buckingham and Coffman 1999, p. 23).

Both standardized tests and professional judgment are necessary. The limitations of standardized tests have been well documented. Similarly, the subjective nature of professional judgments, even when free of unacceptable bias, underscores their obvious limitations. To appreciate the limitations of subjective judgments, one only needs to consider the controversy frequently generated by the judging panels for figure skating and other Olympic events. However, rather than discard them entirely, both standardized tests and professional judgment should be used in a limited and judicious way.

Students in our democracy do not need to pass a test for citizenship. In a few years all of them, regardless of how well they did in school, will be eligible to vote and serve on juries. The democratic ideal does not promote second-class citizens, and implementation of the civic standard can move public schools closer to that ideal.

Broadening the scope of assessment for participatory values makes the task of public education more difficult, but there are rewards. For students and educators, education should be more interesting. The educator's role as a professional is enhanced with the increased need for professional judgment. In addition to developing skills and values important to preserving and strengthening our constitutional democracy, a broader range of students can be expected to do well in school if participatory values are given as much emphasis as cognitive skills currently are given; and these benefits are not limited by race, language, or gender. While the best students will continue to do well in both cognitive and participatory domains, many students who currently are overlooked and undervalued can still do well in public schools if their participatory skills and accomplishments are recognized and valued. Unlike the free-enterprise economic model, which emphasizes competition more than cooperation, the civic standard shifts the balance toward greater cooperation and broader values.

Civic Engagement

The participation called for by the civic standard is not limited to classroom discussion. It provides a rationale for a broad range of extracurricular and community programs. Preparing students to participate actively within their schools and communities develops their participatory skills and values and makes it more likely that they will be able to participate effectively to improve their children's schools in the future. While most public schools already allocate substantial resources to extracurricular activities, some schools may need to reevaluate the purpose of such participation given the civic standard.

For example, athletic programs often convey the message that "winning isn't everything, it's the only thing." Such a message could be defended if the founders had conceived the primary purpose of public education as training for a free-market economy, but another sports adage is more appropriate for public schools given the civic standard: "It's not whether you win or lose, but how you play the game."

Many schools already have implemented service learning and other community participation programs.

Given the long history of vaguely defined and often conflicting versions of citizenship, it should not be surprising that these programs also reflect different interpretations of good citizenship. In reviewing various service learning programs that talk about developing citizens for our democracy, Joseph Kahne and Joel Westheimer underscore the differences between programs that equate good citizenship with charity (such as character education and "a thousand points of light") rather than change (critical analysis and collective social action). Kahne and Westheimer conclude: "Citizenship in a democratic community requires more than kindness and decency; it requires engagement in complex social and institutional endeavors. . . . Citizenship requires that individuals work to create, evaluate, criticize, and change public institutions and programs" (Kahne and Westheimer 1996, p. 597).

Kahne and Westheimer provide a helpful description of conservative versus liberal forms of citizenship programs, but their apparent political preference for the latter is not consistent with the civic standard. A critical analysis of "complex social endeavors," for example, does not necessarily lead to the conclusion that change is always preferable to the status quo. The civic standard provides a framework for students to analyze, consider, and debate the issues before reaching their own conclusions about the best resolution of these differences.

The civic standard clearly goes beyond individual acts of charity or simple book-learning about citizenship in a democracy. It emphasizes not only participation, but effective participation. Critical analysis is essential to a viable democracy, but what is "effective" should remain an open question. Critical analysis could have a conservative or a liberal focus. But it leaves open the question of the best approach to social issues.

Professional Commitment

While much time and debate is focused on the best education philosophy for a school, most parents would rather have their children educated by committed, well-educated teachers regardless of their philosophy. No matter how consistent with the school's mission statement a teacher's stated views are, their children's education will suffer if the educators within the system are not committed to learning and are not well-educated themselves.

Public schools must attract and retain committed, well-educated teachers; but the schools' structure, goals, and practices often make this difficult. For example, the focus on standardized testing to the exclusion of other goals is dispiriting to our best teachers. Some choose to leave, rather than teach to a test; or they respond in other negative ways to the narrowing demands of top-down, mandated testing. The very best teachers stay to do the best they can; they comply with the testing mandates yet try to provide a broader education for their students. Many who stay become dispirited. The problem of public school teachers who start strong and committed only to become dispirited within a few years preceded the current testing movement, but some reports indicate that the testing movement has aggravated the problem. Most educators are skeptical of the top-down mandates that politicians, with help from some corporate executives, are forcing on them in the name of standards and in the form of standardized testing.

Increasing teacher salaries to achieve and retain parity with comparable professional salaries remains an important goal, but the best teachers would go elsewhere if their primary incentive was salary. Their primary goal is the satisfaction that comes with helping children develop to the best of their potential; and this result is more likely, even if more difficult, given the demands of the civic standard.

Citizen Involvement

Just as it takes a village to raise a child, it takes the entire community to prepare a good citizen. To be most effective, a wide range of civic participants need to engage with and support their schools: students, educators, board members, administrators, politicians, and the broader community of citizens of which students are a part.

One study focusing on "civic capacity" in 11 urban school districts in 1993-94 noted that school systems are not well-equipped to deal with broad education issues without a strong foundation of community support (Stone 2001). This is the case even with a highly motivated superintendent because the normal politics of school systems are focused on everyday operations and protecting the status quo. The Stone study contrasts Atlanta, with its loose civic organization, with El Paso, which drew on the major institutional bases of power and resources to bring all segments of the community together. The different ways in which Pittsburgh, Boston, and even Los Angeles created strong versions of comprehensive coalitions are examined. The Stone study concludes: "To be lasting, civic capacity needs an institutional foundation for interaction among elites and a 'grassroots' base through which ordinary citizens are engaged" (p. 595).

Some studies conclude that broad community participation is the key factor in school reform and improved student performance. These studies underscore the importance of public schools emphasizing participatory values because the quality of schools for future generations depends in large part on the participatory skills and values of their parents.

Conclusion

The civic standard provides a primary direction for public education. While the concept is both conservative and old, full implementation of the civic standard has profound implications. Schools would need to reevaluate not only the content of their curricula, but also the process and structure of education to determine if they are designed well enough to achieve the primary civic standard. Since most schools have many purposes and do not have a clear sense of primary purpose, significant changes may need to be made. For some this will be sufficient reason to oppose full implementation of the civic standard, but others will welcome its potential for meaningful change.

A primary purpose is not a sole purpose. The civic standard does not preclude other purposes. Academic, economic, and other purposes can be incorporated in the civic standard. Some of these secondary purposes will serve the primary purpose indirectly, and others will merely not obstruct that purpose. However, if the various purposes of education conflict, it is the civic standard that should prevail.

Education reformers and critics might dismiss the civic standard because it is nothing new and because it simply incorporates the status quo. In one sense, they would be correct. The civic standard is less a reform of education than it is a return to the original purpose for public education as conceived more than 200 years ago. While the concept is deeply rooted in our history, the civic standard has significant implications for the structure, content, and process of public education today. It is idealistic in that it focuses on the core values central to our Constitution and history. It is realistic in that it also focuses on the shortcomings of our constitutional democracy: the gap between those lofty values and everyday practice, numerous imperfections, and unresolved problems. It is full of promise because it provides the cognitive skills and participatory values that our future citizens will need to effect change and start to close the gap between theory and practice. In sum, the civic standard, if implemented, means that students will be better prepared to participate effectively as citizens in our constitutional democracy.

References

Bailey, Susan McGee, and the American Association of University Women (AAUW). *How Schools Shortchange Girls*. New York: Marlowe & Company, 1995.

Buckingham, Marcus, and Coffman, Curt. *First, Break All The Rules: What the World's Greatest Managers Do Differently*. New York: Simon and Schuster, 1999.

Cressman, George R., and Benda, Harold W. *Public Education in America*. New York: Foundation Press, 1960.

Gardner, Howard. *Multiple Intelligences: The Theory in Practice*. New York: Basic Books, 1993.

Gelhorn, Walter, and Byse, Clark. *Administrative Law: Cases and Comments*. New York: Foundation Press, 1960.

Gutmann, Amy. *Democratic Education*. Princeton, New Jersey: Princeton University Press, 1999.

Kahne, Joseph, and Westheimer, Joel. "In the Service of What? The Politics of Service Learning." *Phi Delta Kappan* 77 (May 1996): p. 593-99.

McClung, Merle. "Miles College: A Chance for Birmingham's Black Students?" *American Oxonian* 57 (April 1970): 348-54.

Putnam, Robert D. *Bowling Alone: The Collapse and Revival of American Community*. New York: Simon and Schuster, 2000.

Ravitch, Diane. *Left Back: A Century of Failed School Reform*. New York: Simon and Schuster, 2000.

Rebell, Michael A. "Education Adequacy, Democracy and the Courts." In *Achieving High Educational Standards for All*, edited by Christopher Edley et al. New York: National Academy Press, 2002.

Ryan, James E. "Schools, Race, and Money." *Yale Law Journal* 109 (1999): 249-316.

Sizer, Theodore R. *Horace's Compromise: The Dilemma of the American High School*. Boston: Houghton Mifflin, 1984.

Stone, Clarence N. "Civic Capacity and Urban Education." *Urban Affairs Review* 36 (May 2001): 595-619.

Tucker, Marc. "The Roots of Backlash: A Midterm Assessment of the Standards and Accountability Movement." *Education Week*, 9 January 2002, pp. 7-6.

Court Cases

Brown v. *Board of Education*, 347 U.S. 483 (1954).

Campaign for Fiscal Equity v. *State*, 655 N.E.2d 661 (NY 1995).

Campaign for Fiscal Equity v. *State*, 719 N.Y.S.2d 475 (NY SupCt. 2001).

San Antonio Independent School District v. *Rodriguez*, 411 U.S. 1 (1973).

West Virginia Board of Education v. *Barnette*, 319 U.S. 483 (1943).

Recent Books Published by the
Phi Delta Kappa Educational Foundation

**A Digest of Supreme Court Decisions
Affecting Education, Fourth Edition**
Perry A. Zirkel
Trade paperback. $32.95 (PDK members, $24.95)
CD-ROM edition.* $69.95 (PDK members, $52.95)
Set (1 book, 1 CD) $87.95 (PDK members, $69.95)
*CD is compatible for PCs and Macs.

**Flying with Both Wings:
Inventing the Past to Teach the Future**
Neil Brewer
Trade paperback. $17.95 (PDK members, $13.95)

Environmental Education: A Resource Handbook
Joe E. Heimlich
Trade paperback. $22.95 (PDK members, $17.95)

**Care for Young Children in
Four English-Speaking Countries**
Jo Ann Belk et al.
Trade paperback. $17.95 (PDK members, $13.95)

Psychology of Success
Emery Stoops
Trade paperback. $14.95 (PDK members, $11.95)

Tutor Quest
Edward E. Gordon
Trade paperback. $10.95 (PDK members, $8.95)

Use Order Form on Next Page Or Phone 1-800-766-1156

*A processing charge is added to all orders.
Prices are subject to change without notice.*

Complete online catalog at http://www.pdkintl.org

Order Form

SHIP TO:

STREET

CITY/STATE OR PROVINCE/ZIP OR POSTAL CODE

DAYTIME PHONE NUMBER	PDK MEMBER ROLL NUMBER

QUANTITY	TITLE	PRICE

ORDERS MUST INCLUDE PROCESSING CHARGE

Total Merchandise	Processing Charge
Up to $50	$5
$50.01 to $100	$10
More than $100	$10 plus 5% of total

Special shipping available upon request.
Prices subject to change without notice.

SUBTOTAL	
Indiana residents add 5% Sales Tax	
PROCESSING CHARGE	
TOTAL	

☐ Payment Enclosed (check payable to Phi Delta Kappa International)

Bill my ☐ VISA ☐ MasterCard ☐ American Express ☐ Discover

ACCT #   DATE

			/				

EXP DATE   SIGNATURE

Mail or fax your order to: Phi Delta Kappa International,
P.O. Box 789, Bloomington, IN 47402-0789. USA
Fax: (812) 339-0018. Phone: (812) 339-1156

For fastest service, phone 1-800-766-1156 and use your credit card.